To Mary
From Bonnie

Some people come into our lives, touch our hearts, and we are forever changed. I dedicate this book to my dear friends Elisa, Dawn and Amy; and to my best friend and husband, Ross.

Sue Fitzpatrick Cornelison
Illustrator

You've Been an Angel to Me!™ —*In Celebration of Friends*
copyright © 1997 Landauer Books,
a division of Landauer Corporation,
12251 Maffitt Road, Cumming, Iowa 50061

President and Publisher: Jeramy Lanigan Landauer
Editor: Becky Johnston
Illustrator: Sue Fitzpatrick Cornelison
Design: Nicole Bratt
Technical Production: Roxanne LeMoine
Prepress: Event Graphics
Printed in Hong Kong.

All rights reserved. No part of this book may be reproduced or transmitted in any form or by any means, electronic or mechanical, including, photocopying, recording, or by any information storage and retrieval system without permission in writing from the publisher. Any commercial use of this book by dismantling, or selling prints framed or unframed, or using any part for any form of reproduction is strictly prohibited. While every effort has been made to trace copyright holders, the publisher would be pleased to hear from any not acknowledged.

This book is printed on acid-free paper.

ISBN: 0964-6870-5-4

10 9 8 7 6 5 4 3 2 1
First Edition

Other Books in the You've Been an Angel to Me!™ Series:
In Celebration of Angels
In Celebration of Love

You've Been an Angel to Me!™

In Celebration of

Friends

ILLUSTRATIONS BY SUE FITZPATRICK CORNELISON
VERSE BY BECKY JOHNSTON

LANDAUER BOOKS
LANDAUER CORPORATION
CUMMING, IOWA

When an acquaintanceship blossoms into a deep and abiding friendship, it is indeed a miracle to behold and an inexplicable joy to experience. It is as though the glories of Heaven have truly come to earth...as the miracle of friendship unfolds, it is surely the greatest evidence that a friend in need can be an angel indeed!

Becky Johnston
Editor

What is a friend?

A single soul dwelling in two bodies.

Aristotle

Friendship is something that raises us almost

above humanity…It is the sort of love

one can imagine between angels.

C.S. Lewis

*W*hen is a friend

most like an angel?

Being with you is like walking

on a very clear morning—

definitely the sensation of belonging there.

E.B. White

I am so glad you are here…It helps me

to realize how beautiful my world is.

Rainer Maria Rilke

No love, no friendship can cross the path

of our destiny without leaving

some mark on it forever.

François Mauriac

A friend, like an angel,

treats every day

as a great beginning…

I always felt that the great high privilege,
relief and comfort of friendship was that
one had to explain nothing.

Katherine Mansfield

Friendship: It involves many things, but,
above all, the power of going out of one's self
and seeing and appreciating whatever is
noble and loving in another.

Thomas Hughes

A friend, like an angel, forgetting the worst, remembers only the best…

The better part of one's life consists
of one's friendships.

Abraham Lincoln

Friend derives from a word meaning "free."
A friend is someone who allows us
the space and freedom to be.

Debbie Alicen

Friends, books, cheerful heart,
and conscience clear are the most choice
companions we have here.

William Mather

A friend, like an angel, accepts our limitations…

No one can develop freely in this world
and find a full life without feeling understood
by at least one person.

Paul Tournier

You have done it without a touch.

Without a word, without a sign.

You have done it by being yourself.

Perhaps that is what being a friend is.

Roy Croft

A friend, like an angel,

shares our hope of making

dreams come true…

But friendship is precious, not only in
the shade, but in the sunshine of life;
and thanks to a benevolent arrangement
of things, the greater part of life is sunshine.

Thomas Jefferson

If we would build on a sure foundation
in friendship, we must love our friends
for their sakes rather than our own.

Charlotte Brontë

A friend,

like an angel,

gives the gift

of hope…

Don't walk in front of me, I may not follow.
Don't walk behind me, I may not lead.
Walk beside me and just be my friend.
Albert Camus

To know someone here or there with whom
you feel there is an understanding in spite
of distances or thoughts unexpressed—
that can make of this earth a garden.
Goethe

A friend, like an angel, respects our differences…

Friendship is like love at its best:
not blind but sympathetically all-seeing;
a support which does not wait
for understanding;
an act of faith
which does not need,
but always has, reason.

Louis Untermeyer

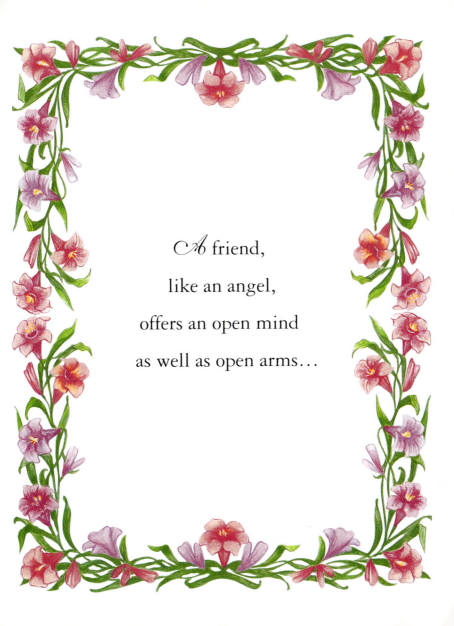

A friend,

like an angel,

offers an open mind

as well as open arms…

It is easy to say how we love new friends,
and what we think of them,
but words can never trace out
all the fibers that knit us to the old.

George Eliot

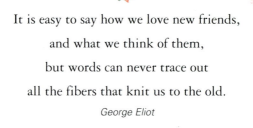

If instead of a gem or even a flower,
we should cast the gift of a lovely thought
into the heart of a friend, that would be
giving even as an angel gives.

George MacDonald

A friend,

like an angel,

plants seeds of love

for us to nurture…

We are so very rich if we know just a few people in a way in which we know no others.

Catherine Bramwell-Booth

What the heart gives away is never gone…
It is kept in the hearts of others.

Robin St. John

A friend, like an angel,

lifts even the heaviest

of hearts…

There's something beautiful about finding
one's innermost thoughts in another.

Oliver Schreiner

The glory of friendship is not the
outstretched hand, nor the kindly smile
nor the joy of companionship; it is the
spirited inspiration that comes to one
when one discovers that someone else
believes and is willing to entrust
their friendship.

Ralph Waldo Emerson

$\mathscr{A}$ friend, like an angel,

lends us wings so we can find

our way home…

A friend may well be reckoned

the masterpiece of nature.

Ralph Waldo Emerson

We cannot tell the precise moment
when a friendship starts…
It is like filling a vessel drop-by-drop
which makes it at last run over;
so a series of kindnesses…
make the heart run over.

James Boswell

My friends are my estate.

Emily Dickinson

A friend, like an angel,
is like a fragrant flower
in the garden of life…

A friend, like an angel,

is always there for us…

Thanks for always being there,

my friend…

You've been an angel to me!

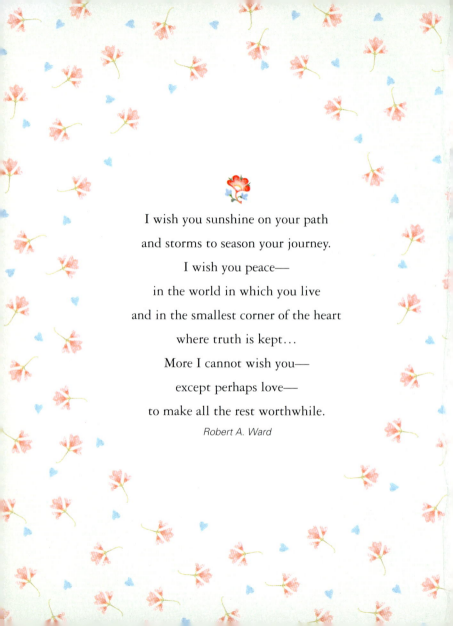

I wish you sunshine on your path

and storms to season your journey.

I wish you peace—

in the world in which you live

and in the smallest corner of the heart

where truth is kept…

More I cannot wish you—

except perhaps love—

to make all the rest worthwhile.

Robert A. Ward